Grow Your Stock Exchange with Futures and Options

Grow Your Stock Exchange with Futures and Options

A Guide to Understanding These Financial Instruments

CHARLIE RUBIN

Grow Your Stock Exchange with Futures and Options: A Guide to Understanding These Financial Instruments

Copyright © 2009 Charlie Rubin. All rights reserved. No part of this book may be reproduced or retransmitted in any form or by any means without the written permission of the publisher.

Published by Wheatmark®
610 East Delano Street, Suite 104
Tucson, Arizona 85705 U.S.A.
www.wheatmark.com

International Standard Book Number: 978-1-60494-281-1
Library of Congress Control Number: 2009926346

The author can be reached at crubinfutures@yahoo.com

www.GrowYourStockExchange.com

To my wife, Nan, who inspired me to write this book.

Contents

About the Author ix

Introduction 1
Chapter 1: The Basics 7
Chapter 2: Futures. 15
Chapter 3: Hedgers and Speculators 27
Chapter 4: Hedging Stock Portfolios 37
Chapter 5: Hedging Debt Portfolios. 41
Chapter 6: Pre-positioning for Asset Managers. 45
Chapter 7: Other Hedging and Spread Trading
    Applications. 49
Chapter 8: FCMs and IBs. 57

Chapter 9: How Futures Operate 59
Chapter 10: Margin. 65
Chapter 11: Overview of IT Implications for Trading and
    Settlement of Derivatives on Stock Exchanges 71
Chapter 12: Developing Leveraged Products 75
Chapter 13: Options 79
Chapter 14: Option Operations. 85
Chapter 15: Option Pricing. 89
Chapter 16: Trading and Benefits of Options. 93
Chapter 17: Hedging with Options 101
Chapter 18: Options Helping the Farmer and the
    People. 107
Chapter 19: Review of Uses and Choices 111
Chapter 20: Recommendations for Moving Onward . . . 115

About the Author

Charlie Rubin has served as CEO for stock and futures brokerage firms. He has held senior management positions at stock and futures exchanges, and was responsible for the modification of the New York Stock Exchange settlement system that became the settlement system for the New York Futures Exchange. Over the past 15 years, Mr. Rubin has consulted on a variety of securities and commodity derivative projects in many emerging countries. This has included providing workshops on futures and options that correlate to the contents of this book. His work continues with stock and commodity exchanges, including enhancing trading and settlement systems to accommodate futures and options; and to revise customer recordkeeping and accounting systems to include these derivatives transactions.

He has created this informative, easy to understand book and welcomes your feedback.

Charlie Rubin

Former vice president, New York Futures Exchange
Director, SIAC (Securities Industry Automation Corporation), division of New York Stock Exchange
CEO, Deak Perara Futures, Inc.
CEO, Deak Perera Securities, Inc.
CEO, HSN Securities, Inc.
BA and BS, Columbia University
Guest lecturer, New York University Business School
Securities and derivatives professional licenses: Series 3, 7, 27, 28

Email: crubinfutures@yahoo.com

www.GrowYourStockExchange.com

Introduction

Futures and options have been shown to enhance the activity of stock exchange products and greatly expand financial offerings. In the U.S., the introduction of stock index futures resulted in daily trading activity rising from millions to billions of shares. In India, by introducing stock and stock index futures, a fairly new stock exchange became the third most active exchange in the world. This is something other stock exchanges should be doing; not just for financial futures, but for futures in the more traditional commodities (e.g., wheat, coffee, cotton, crude oil, etc.). In many countries, the people and the economy are more closely associated with these traditional commodities. The major reason why futures are not traded is the general lack of knowledge about these financial instruments.

This book only describes exchange traded derivatives—futures and options—how they operate, their similarities and differences, and how they compare with stock trading and settlement operations. These derivatives are regulated with position limits, margin requirements, and price limits (all of which are subsequently described). The non-regulated, non-exchange-traded or over–the-counter derivatives, such as credit default swaps, which led to the worldwide financial crises in 2008, are excluded from this discussion.

Frank Partnoy, well-known author of "*Infectious Greed*", has written extensively about the detrimental effects of non-regulated derivatives and provided expert testimony to the U.S. Senate investigating this subject. He states: "The two basic types of derivatives, options and futures, were traded on regulated exchanges and enabled parties to reduce or refocus their risks in ways that improved the overall efficiency of the economy."

The material in this book is both introductory and comprehensive. It begins with working definitions for derivatives and commodities, as well as cash and futures markets. Upon completion, the reader will understand these financial instruments, their many uses, benefits, and risks.

Futures and options should be understood by stock exchange, depository, brokerage firm, and government regulator personnel. While the industry benefits via fees and commissions, so do their institutional and retail customers.

All customers are either hedgers or speculators. Hedgers want to *reduce or eliminate* financial risks in the marketplace; and speculators *take* financial risks in order to achieve profits.

An entire book could be written on the applications of futures and options for hedging against price increases or decreases. In some countries, hedging is known as "insurance." For example, hedgers can be wheat farmers, who want to protect against a price decrease of their wheat crop; or food wholesalers, who want to protect against a price increase of wheat. Companies, too, can hedge currency fluctuation and interest rate risks. Likewise, institutional and retail customers who want to protect or reduce the risk of their securities portfolio can do so with stock index futures and options.

For financial and other commodity speculators, these derivatives are ideal because of the leverage that is inherent in them and the trading and investment diversity they offer. Anyone who has ever bought a stock, a bond, or a mutual fund is a speculator. The amount of risk will vary, but people buy securities because they think or expect that the price will go higher, and therefore make a profit. However, if the price declines, they will incur a monetary loss. That's speculation. Even when purchasing a bond and holding it to maturity, there is the risk that the issuer may not make all of the principal and interest payments. There is a myth that futures have greater volatility and risk than stocks. This book will explain how futures carry the same risk and volatility as stocks or other commodities traded in the cash markets.

Another area included in this book is the similarities and differences between stock and derivative trading and settlement operations. The basic functional revisions necessary for stock exchange and depository systems to accommodate futures and options are described along with other requirements (e.g., contract selection, training, etc.) for implementation.

There is discussion of how futures and options allow investors / customers to buy / sell individual securities or an entire market (index) with leverage, make no interest payments, and do so with no downside or market risk. Likewise, the author demonstrates how to utilize these derivatives to buy securities below the market or "at a discount," generate additional revenue and interest income, and take advantage of narrowing or widening long and short term interest rate spreads.

Additionally, this book shows how futures and options allow retail and institutional investors to hedge or reduce their market, interest rate, and currency risks. These derivatives allow investors to protect their positions against market price declines while still maintaining their dividends and other corporate actions, and to become fully invested without full market risk. By using these derivatives, pension fund managers (or any asset managers who receive regular contributions) may take advantage of market conditions by investing when they think appropriate, even before the fund contributions are made.

Actual examples throughout help the reader better understand the information. After finishing this book, the reader should comprehend what these derivative products are and how they operate. The reader should also grasp the impact and potential magnitude that these financial products can have on investors, financial and commodity industries, and the economic and social well-being of an entire country.

Chapter 1

The Basics

What is a commodity?

That's an easy question. The answer is, practically everything. Stocks are financial commodities. So are long- and short-term debt instruments (e.g., bonds). Stock and bond indices are commodities. So are currencies, metals (e.g., gold, silver, platinum), and various grades of oil products. Of course there are the traditional agricultural commodities, such as wheat, corn, cotton, sugar, etc., etc.

What is a derivative?

A dictionary will define a derivative as something that is taken or derived from something else. That was easy. In our context, a derivative is a financial instrument that is related to or derived from any underlying commodity. As mentioned in the Introduction, the only derivatives we will discuss are futures and options of commodities that are traded on regulated exchanges.

Cash and Futures markets

There are two types of markets: Cash (or Spot) markets and Futures markets.

In a *Cash market*, after you buy or sell something such as a stock, the settlement of that trade—where the seller delivers the commodity to the buyer and the buyer pays the seller—happens on the same day, within a few days, or even within a week or two. All of these time frames are considered Cash market transactions.

"Cash market" and "Spot market" are synonymous. Stock markets are Cash markets.

In *Futures markets*, the delivery of the underlying commodity is in the future—perhaps three or six months, or even more than one year. The exact delivery time is stated in the standardized contract specifications for that commodity.

All commodities may be traded in the Cash market and the Futures market. In our context, the only Cash market commodities that are traded on regulated exchanges are securities. Other commodities that trade in the Cash or Spot market usually do not do so on regulated exchanges. However, commodity futures are traded on regulated exchanges, so this book deals will all of these commodity futures.

"Commodity exchange," "derivative exchange," and "futures exchange" are all synonymous. Most of the time these exchanges are called futures exchanges, but sometimes they are referred to as derivative or commodity exchanges. One exchange, the largest one in India, has both commodity and derivative in its name. All futures exchanges trade futures, and some trade options on their futures contracts.

It is important to understand that for trades in the Cash market (on stock exchanges), the seller and buyer are obligated to make and take delivery on settlement date.

The following terminology is the same for trading and positions on stock exchanges and futures exchanges. When a customer initially buys, he owns the stock or commodity and has a "long position." A "long sale" refers to a sale from a long position. A "short sale" refers to a sale of a stock or commodity that the seller does not own, and creates a "short position."

For trades on futures exchanges, a buyer or seller may liquidate his long or short position prior to the delivery settlement, and therefore not participate in that commodity delivery. Of course, if buyers or sellers on futures exchanges liquidate their position prior to the delivery date(s), they are still obligated or responsible for any profits or losses between the price at the time the trade is executed and the price at the time when that position is liquidated.

Options are financial derivatives, more complex than futures, which are traded on stock exchanges and futures exchanges. We have exchanges that specialize in options, such as the Chicago Board of Options Exchange (CBOE), that trade options on stocks that are listed on other stock exchanges.

I trust this clears up the confusion in terminology of commodities, derivatives, futures markets and exchanges, stock exchanges, options exchanges, and spot or cash markets.

Some basic concepts

There are some basic conceptual similarities and differences in the trading and settlement operations between stock exchanges and futures exchanges, and between their respective depositories.

Trade date/settlement date

Let's first look at the concept of trade date and settlement date. For both exchanges, the trade date is the same—the day that a trade is executed or a commitment is made.

On stock exchanges, the settlement of the trade (the exchange of securities and money) takes place usually within 1 to 5 days in line with international best practices. The actual settlement procedures of the various depositories vary widely, but basically, the broker representing the seller delivers the securities through the depository to the broker representing the buyer, who pays the full value (quantity of the security multiplied by the transaction price) of the delivery.

On futures exchanges, the delivery of the contractual obligation takes place "in the future," sometimes many months away. In order to make sure that adverse price movements do not result in significant market losses (to the buyer/long position or the seller/short position), the Clearing Members must make a "good-faith deposit" or margin deposit on behalf of their customers.[1] Daily, every trade and position held is "marked to market." The "mark to market" generates an unrealized profit or loss for that trade or position. The margin deposit is based upon the size of the position and the unrealized profit or loss in each position held. The exact margin requirement amounts are stipulated in the commodity contract specifications.

In all transactions, there is settlement risk. That risk or exposure to nonpayment exists for the time between trade date and settlement date. Therefore, a shorter time frame is safer because there's less settlement risk. The risk is that one of the brokerages in a trade (usually the broker representing the buyer) goes out of business or does not have the funds to pay for the securities (or commodity). For the stock market, the settlement time frame is usually anywhere from 1 to 5 days. With exchange-traded derivatives, all brokerages

---

[1] It's the customer's obligation to make the margin deposit to his broker/clearing member. The clearing member is responsible for making the margin deposit to the depository. I will discuss this in more detail later.

representing both the buy side and sell side must make the required margin deposit the following morning before trading begins. Unless this occurs, the broker would usually not be allowed any further trading, and his positions would be liquidated. Therefore, for futures and options, the settlement risk is limited to overnight.

This margin concept should not be confused with a customer buying a stock in a separate margin account with his broker. In this situation, the broker finances part of the customer purchase and charges the customer interest for the financed amount or debit balance. With futures, this concept of financing and interest charges does not exist.

Short selling

Another major difference between operations and rules on stock exchanges and futures exchanges involves short selling. Short selling involves selling a security or any commodity that the seller does not own at the time of sale.

With securities, "short sales" are executed in a separate account (from a customer cash account or margin account), and the sell order must be so identified. In some countries, short selling is not even permitted. On the settlement date, the securities sold must be delivered (otherwise creating a "fail to deliver"), so the securities must be borrowed, requiring lending/borrowing mechanisms among the brokers to be in place. Where short selling is permitted, there may also be rules that require price increases for a short sale to take place.

With futures trading, none of the above restrictions or rules apply. There is no distinction between a long sell order and a short sell order. The concept of borrowing securities to make a delivery does not exist. Every sell execution will either reduce a long position or create a short position.

Aside from having more trading vehicles in which a customer may generate profits, the trading rules for these derivatives create many more opportunities for customers to make profits. In trading or investing, the object is to buy low and sell high (always a good strategy). On stock exchanges that do not permit short selling, or where securities are not available for borrowing, the only way for a customer to make a profit is if he first buys a stock. If he's correct and the stock price goes higher, he'll have a profit. If a customer thinks the price of a stock will go down, he cannot take advantage of this situation since he cannot "go short," or sell first. This is not the case with futures. With no short selling restrictions, a customer may buy or sell first, depending upon which way he thinks the price will go.

Electronic trading versus Open Outcry

In the U.S., where commodity or futures trading has existed for a very long time, in contrast to computerized or electronic matched trading, trading takes place on a trading floor in a "trading pit" under a procedure known as "Open

Outcry." This is the scene that we see on television when the news concerns major price increases or decreases in various commodities. Without getting into a full description of the details, in an Open Outcry environment orders can be relatively easily manipulated by the floor members. Thus, rather than benefiting customers, this type of trading environment greatly benefits the floor members, who are the exchange owners, and therefore perpetuate and enjoy the continuation of this trading procedure.

For recently established commodity exchanges, and certainly for developing countries, the same computer order entry and matching model that is used for stock trading should be utilized for futures trading. The changes or modifications to a computer stock trading system that would be required to accommodate derivative trading are not significantly difficult to program. Modifications to the settlement system are more involved. Later chapters in this book will identify these modifications.

There are continuing efforts to standardize some of the aspects of derivative procedures on an international basis.

Since options are more complex and complicated than futures, we'll start with the subject of futures.

CHAPTER 2

Futures

What is a future?

A future is a financial instrument representing a standardized contract of an underlying commodity that is bought or sold for delivery versus payment at a future date—the expiration of the contract. That purchase or sale (long or short) position may be liquidated before expiration of the contract.

At the expiration of each commodity contract, the resultant long and short positions participate in the delivery and payment of the underlying commodity.

As with a stock transaction, a futures trade and resultant position is a firm commitment. It is not an option, where you have a choice of whether or not you want to make or take delivery. As with stocks, if you buy a futures contract and the price increases, you have an unrealized profit. If the price decreases, you have an unrealized loss. Also, if you sell a futures contract and incur a short position, and the price increases, you have an unrealized loss. If the price decreases, you have an unrealized profit.

Futures contract

All elements of commodities traded are defined and stipulated in the standard futures contract. The contracts are determined by the exchange, and approved by the government regulator.

The trading quantity is in number of contracts, and not in number of shares as it is for stock trades.

There are several elements of a futures contract:

Commodity name: This is the name of the commodity (e.g., gold).

Quantity of the underlying commodity. For example, the contract may be for 100 ounces of gold, 100 shares of a specific stock, 1,000 barrels of crude oil, $100,000 of par value of a government bond, 37,500 pounds of coffee, 5,000 bushels of corn, 5,000 bushels of wheat, 125,000 euros, etc.

- The value of a commodity contract is the quantity of the contract amount multiplied by the price. For example, if a crude oil contract trades at 40 USD (US dollars) per barrel, then the contract value is 1,000 × 40 = 40,000 USD

Grade of the underlying commodity. Where appropriate, the contract would stipulate a specific grade, such as the fineness for a gold contract or the sulfur level of a crude oil contract.

Contract months. This identifies the expiration month of the contract. For example, many of the financial contracts (e.g., stock index contracts) expire on a quarterly basis, with the contract expiration months being March, June, September, and December.

- Regarding trading and settlement operations, each contract month for the same commodity is treated as a separate entity, just as each stock is treated as a separate entity on a stock exchange.

Expiration of the contract. For a particular contract month, the expiration or last trading day of that contract is stipulated. It may be stipulated as the last business day of the month, the fourth Thursday of the month, the third Friday of the month, etc. The delivery day is also stated. Usually, the delivery day is the same day or next day after the expiration of trading. (With certain commodities, there may be more than one delivery day). This is when the seller delivers the underlying commodity to the buyer. The payment is determined by the final settlement price of that commodity contract multiplied by the contract quantity. At expiration, the futures market price equals (or closely replicates) the cash market price of the underlying commodity. In the case of a stock index future, the expiration or final settlement price will be the exact value of that underlying stock index.

Contract deliverable. The contract will stipulate whether the deliverable is Physical (the underlying commodity) or Cash.

- For some futures contracts such as stock index futures, the delivery is always in *Cash*. What this really means is that the final positions are "marked" to the final settlement price, which is that day's closing stock index price. The brokers or clearing members representing the buyers and sellers settle to this amount with the depository. As we'll see later, even where there is a physical underlying commodity (such as a stock, wheat, oil, etc.), you will still achieve hedging benefits via a Cash delivery contract.

- Where the deliverable is the underlying *Physical* commodity, the depository will match or pair-off the net buyers and sellers. The sellers deliver the contact quantity and grade of the underlying commodity to the buyers for payment. Some contracts, such as those for agricultural commodities, may state specific delivery sites and warehouses.

Daily price limit. This stipulates the valid price trading range for each day. It limits the daily maximum price change, thus avoiding large daily price swings. It may be simply a percentage change from the previous day's closing or settlement price. For example, if the daily price limit is 5%, then no trade may occur more than 5% or less than 5% from the previous day's settlement price. Daily price limits may also exist on stock exchanges. Although the determination of daily price limits may be subjective, such as 5%, there are well-established, publicly available mathematical and volatility (beta analysis) algorithms and services that may be used to determine daily price limits.

Minimum trading tick. Some contracts may have minimum trading ticks, which means that any price change up or down from the previous trade must be at least a certain minimum amount.

Position limits. Position limits, which vary for each commodity, as defined in the contract specifications, are imposed to prevent any customer or broker from obtaining an "undue concentration" or large position (long or short) of any single commodity. If any customer or broker could obtain such a large position, there would be a greater chance of price manipulation, or even a cornering of the market.

Position limits, both for long and short positions, are expressed as a percentage of the number of contracts outstanding or Open Interest, which is defined later.

- For brokers, position limits would include the total number of contracts for all of their customer accounts, and as an order of magnitude, the limit could approximate 15% to 20%.

- For customers, all related accounts (such as a spouse's account, joint accounts, etc.) should be considered as a single account, and the limit could be approximately 3% to 4%.

- There should be broker and customer position limits for each commodity month and for the total of all months for each commodity.

Margins. This topic is more fully discussed in a later section. It is introduced at this time because it is part of the contract specifications. Margins or margin deposits are required for all futures trades and positions maintained. It is designed to make sure that there is always equity in a long or short futures account, thereby preventing a customer or brokerage firm from "walking away" from its position. Margin requirements are calculated at least daily, in accordance with that day's commodity settlement price. There may be intra-day margin calculations as well.

The exchange may change any aspect or element of any commodity contract, with the approval of the government regulator.

Some properties of futures versus stocks

Types of orders: Order types are determined by the exchange. Basically, the types of orders for futures would be the same as for stocks—for instance, market orders, limit orders, GTC orders, etc.

- However, because of the technical trading strategies (as opposed to fundamental trading strategies) utilized with futures, any futures trading system should or even must have Stop orders, and better yet, Stop limit orders. Technical strategies plot and project commodity prices based upon price and volume patterns, and having the ability to limit a loss, take a profit, or establish a position while trading many futures contracts at the same time is greatly enhanced by utilizing Stop orders. Examples of using Stop orders are described in a later chapter.

- As stated earlier, with futures, there is no special designation between long sale and short sale orders. All sell orders are accepted in the same manner that buy orders are accepted into the trading system.

Settlement price. This can be the same methodology as the determination of the settlement price (or closing price) of a stock on a stock exchange. However, for margin purposes, all futures trades and positions are valued to this settlement price each day, so the determination of this price is critical.

The settlement price should reflect the "end of day" price and therefore the value of each commodity contract. With electronic systems, this is a rather routine and objective task. For example, the settlement price may be the weighted average of all contracts traded within the final 15 minutes of trading. This time period is referred to as the Closing Range, and market orders may be designated as Market on Close (MOC) orders, but more about that later. (For each commodity, each contract month will have its own settlement price).

In the U.S., which utilizes the "manual" system of Open Outcry, the determination of the settlement price is more subjective. The exchange's Floor Governors determine the settlement price more subjectively after their review and discussion of trading during the Closing Range.

Futures deliveries

At expiration of a futures contract, delivery is made by all remaining sellers to buyers versus payment. There are two issues here. Is the delivery cash or physical, and what price does the buyer pay? There is no choice for the buyer or seller because the contract specifications ("specs") define the delivery mechanism.

Deliveries

Typically, for some contracts such as agricultural, metal, and oil, the delivery is the actual product ("physical delivery") because the seller is usually a producer (e.g., farmer or oil producer) who wants to make a delivery of his product. Also, the buyer is generally a user (e.g., food wholesaler or oil refinery) who wants to receive the physical product. In these instances, the depository or clearinghouse will pair-off the buyers and sellers for the deliveries, usually based upon size of the delivery and delivery points.

For futures exchanges, the settlement and delivery functions are the responsibility of the clearinghouse, which is associated with the particular exchange. With fully computerized stock exchange trading, there are no clearinghouses. Depositories are associated with the exchanges, and are responsible for trade settlements (the receipt and delivery of securities versus payment). When stock exchanges establish futures and option trading, it should be these depositories that are also responsible for the margin settlement of trades, as well as the delivery functions for these derivative contracts—the same functions performed by clearinghouses for futures exchanges. Therefore, in this book, the terms "clearinghouse" and "depository" are usually interchangeable.

Since stock exchanges don't deal in these actual or physical commodities, it would be appropriate for the exchange (a stock exchange that is now trading futures) to have these commodities deliver for Cash. This means that the final buyers and sellers would be "marked to market" to the cash price for that commodity. The hedgers, as indicated above—the farmer and oil producer, who are the sellers or short hedgers, and the food wholesaler and oil refinery, who are the buyers or long hedgers—would actually make and take delivery in the Spot market versus the prevailing Spot price. The hedger will still have taken advantage of the futures market to hedge or eliminate his price risk because—and this is the essence of the matter—the Cash price that is actually paid and received by the buyer and seller in the Spot market, plus the realized profit or loss on the futures contract position, will equal (with some possible slight variations) the transaction or locked-in price of the futures contract when it was previously bought or sold. We'll see examples of this later.

It should be understood that for speculators, unless the commodity delivery is Cash, their positions should be liquidated prior to the end of trading for those commodity contracts.

For certain contracts a delivery of Cash is the only mechanism that makes sense, such as for stock index futures and bond index futures contracts. For example, a stock index represents an array of round lots, odd lots, and even partial shares of various securities, and it would be inappropriate and extremely difficult to have the sellers actually make delivery of these securities.

Even for delivery of individual stock futures, rather than a physical delivery of the underlying stock, a delivery for Cash eliminates the need to borrow shares and also avoids the possibility of a "short squeeze" if these securities are not readily available for lending.

Delivery price

This is the final settlement price of each contract at the end of the last trading day, and is also the price of the commodity in the Cash or Spot market.

What is this price, and how is it determined?

For some contracts, this is easy. For example, the delivery or final settlement price of a stock index futures contract, such as one for the Standard & Poor's index or an individual stock future, is the exact price or value of that index or the closing price of that stock.

For some contracts, determining the delivery price is more complicated. For example, the Spot price of wheat varies each day, depending upon the delivery points or storage locations of the wheat markets. For these commodities, a mathematical algorithm or formula considering the various locations determine the price. The contract specs state this exact formula, which would certainly affect the futures market price as we approach the end of trading. For contracts where the underlying commodity is to be physically delivered, this price may not be the exact price that the buyer or seller pays or receives for their product in the Spot market. Therefore, although it may not amount to a 100% hedge, depending upon the pricing formula and the actual price paid (or received) in the Spot market, it should represent a hedge or price risk elimination in the high-90s percentile.

Because the final futures contract settlement price is equal to the Cash or Spot price, there is obviously a very close relationship between the futures market and the Cash market. That's why futures are an excellent hedge for users of any underlying commodity. Typically, and it's true for the financial futures, these futures contracts have four expiration dates annually, which means that the futures and spot price will be exactly equal (at least) four times annually. If there are wide price differences or spreads during the trading periods, arbitrageurs will seize the opportunity of locking in profits and narrow the spread.

Open interest

Open Interest is the total number of contracts open or outstanding (long or short) for each contract month, for all commodities. The total number of contracts held in all long positions equals the total number of contracts held in all short positions.

Open Interest is an indication of interest, activity, liquidity, and depth to the market. The higher the Open Interest, the greater the activity and liquidity. Higher Open Interest means tighter spreads and, in general, a better market.

Unlike stocks, there is no primary market for futures. There are no initial public offerings. All futures activity, positions, and Open Interest is created when buyers and sellers agree to a trade via the exchange trading system.

Since the total number of contracts bought, sold, and held in long or short positions are equal, futures are referred to as a "Sum Zero game" (but it's really not a game). It follows that unlike stocks, the total amount of profits made equals the total amount of losses.

When a contract reaches expiration, there is no more trading in that contract month. All open positions are either paired off for physical delivery or settle for cash, and the Open Interest becomes zero.

Chapter 3

Hedgers and Speculators

Simply stated, in the entire world of investing and trading, everyone is either a hedger or a speculator.

Hedgers want to avoid financial risks. In some countries, hedging is referred to as buying insurance.

Speculators want to take financial risks in order to make profits.

Futures markets accommodate both of these groups, and in order to have a long-term viable market, you need both hedgers and speculators.

Using Futures for Speculation

Speculation is not a dirty word. It is a positive and essential ingredient of trading, a contributing factor to the liquidity and price discovery of a market. As stated in the Introduction, anyone who has ever bought a stock, a bond, or a mutual fund has speculated. If the price goes up, you have a profit. If the price goes down, you have a loss. That's speculation.

We should not confuse speculation with leverage and with amount of risk. For example, a stock purchase may be riskier than a bond purchase, but they are both speculative actions.

When you buy something—a stock, a commodity future, etc.—if you don't pay the full purchase price, you have leverage. When you buy a stock on a stock exchange, you pay 100% of the stock value (except for purchases in a margin account). With commodity futures contracts, depending upon the contract specifications, you may have to deposit only 10% (margin) of the contract value. That's leverage.

If you paid 100%, and that stock went up or down 5%, you would have a 5% profit or loss.

However, if you made a 10% margin deposit, and that same stock went up or down 5%, you would have a 50% profit or loss. Big difference. Of course, before your account incurred a major loss and the equity was starting to become minimal, you would receive a margin call to make another cash deposit.

People think futures are very volatile. That is incorrect. They confuse leverage and volatility. The volatility of the cash market and futures are the same; otherwise the futures market would not be used as a hedge for the cash market. Since the delivery price of a futures contract equals the cash market price, the volatility during the contract period is the same.

Suppose you think that the stock market will be going up (or down), but don't know which stocks to buy (or sell short, presuming this is permitted). What you may do is buy (or sell) stock index futures contracts. This way, you'll be able to participate in the overall market move, and be able to have the "action" of 10 times your money deposit (assuming the margin requirement is 10%). That's leverage.

With speculation and hedging, it is easy to see why in many countries, index futures are the most popular and active futures contracts traded.

Using Futures for Hedging

We'll be using examples of participants in the agricultural, oil, and financial sectors to illustrate how futures are used for hedging—to eliminate price or market risk. Farmers and oil producers will establish short hedges (sell futures) to avoid the effects of a drop in their products' prices when it's time to deliver. Food wholesalers and oil users, such as oil refineries or airlines, will establish long hedges (buy futures) to avoid the effects of an increase in the cost of the products that they must buy. For individuals and portfolio managers, we'll see many uses of how to hedge portfolios using futures contracts.

Agriculture—short hedge

Suppose it's March, and a corn farmer is planting corn seeds, which will be harvested and delivered in October. Let's assume that October corn futures contracts are trading at 5 USD per bushel. There are 5,000 bushels of corn per futures contract. The farmer realizes that at 5 USD per bushel he will make a reasonable profit on this year's crop. Sure, he would prefer to sell his corn at a higher price, but would not want to sell at a lower price. By contracting to sell his October delivery of corn at the current October price, 5 USD per bushel, he can lock in that reasonable profit and eliminate the fluctuation in price, or price risk. (If he expects to be selling 10,000 bushels, then he will sell 2 contracts.)

In October, when the corn is harvested and ready for delivery, let's suppose the price of corn has dropped to 3 USD per bushel in the Spot market. Let's also suppose that this exchange has decided to deliver its contracts for Cash (though this really doesn't affect the financial impact). The farmer delivers his corn in the Spot market and receives 3 USD. However, he held a short futures position at 5 USD, and with the final settlement price at 3 USD, he makes a futures trading profit of 2 USD. Therefore, his net selling price is 5 USD, which he locked in back in March. 3 USD (spot sale) + 2 USD (futures trading profit) = net price of 5 USD (per bushel).

What if the price went higher in October? Let's suppose the price of corn has increased to 9 USD per bushel in the Spot market. The farmer delivers his corn in the Spot market and receives 9 USD. However, he held a short futures position at 5 USD, and with the final settlement price at 9 USD, he has incurred a futures trading loss of 4 USD. His net selling price is still 5 USD, which he locked in back in March. 9 USD (spot sale) − 4 USD (futures trading loss) = net price of 5 USD per bushel.

Yes, in the second case, it would have been better for the farmer had he not hedged his delivery price. He would have received the spot price of 9 USD instead of a net of 5 USD. However, that's the point. He eliminated the price risk both up and down, and locked in his reasonable profit in March by selling the October corn futures contract at 5 USD. In fact, if the farmer had thought that the price of corn would increase, and he had been willing to take the risk that he was right, he probably would not have established the hedge.

Agriculture—long hedge

Using the exact same scenario and prices, let's look at the opposite side. Suppose in March (or whenever), a food wholesaler or processor knows he needs to buy corn (to make his corn muffins or whatever) when it is available (at harvest time in October). October corn futures are trading at 5 USD per bushel. The wholesaler realizes that at 5 USD per bushel he will make a reasonable profit. Sure, he would prefer to buy the corn at a lower price, but he would not want to buy it at a higher price. By buying October corn futures contract(s) at the current October price (5 USD), he can lock in that reasonable profit and eliminate the fluctuation in price, or price risk.

Now, in October, when the corn is harvested and ready for purchase, let's suppose the price of corn has dropped to 3 USD per bushel in the Spot market. The wholesaler receives his corn in the Spot market and pays 3 USD. However, he held a long futures position at 5 USD, and with the final settlement price at 3 USD, he incurs a futures trading loss of 2 USD. Therefore, his net purchase price is 5 USD, which he locked in back in March. 3 USD (spot purchase) + 2 USD (futures trading loss) = a net or total cost of 5 USD (per bushel).

Again, what if the price went higher in October? Let's suppose the price of corn has increased to 9 USD (per bushel) in the Spot market. The wholesaler receives his corn in the Spot market and pays 9 USD. However, he held a long futures position at 5 USD, and with the final settlement price at 9 USD, he has a futures trading profit of 4 USD. His net purchase price is still 5 USD, which he previously locked in. 9 USD (Spot market payment) – 4 USD (futures trading profit) = a net cost of 5 USD (per bushel).

As before, if the market price went in his favor, it would have been better for the wholesaler to not have hedged his purchase price. Again, he eliminated the price risk (up or down). Like the farmer, if the wholesaler had thought that the price of corn would go in his favor, and he had been willing to take the risk that he was right, he probably would not have established the hedge.

Oil—short hedge

The concept and actions that an oil producer would take are exactly the same as for the farmer, above. The crude oil producer can also hedge or lock in the selling price of his crude oil.

Of course, there is no harvest time here, and oil is produced all year round. Although several or many months away from contract expiration, let's assume that December oil futures contracts are trading at 75 USD per barrel. The oil producer realizes that at 75 USD per barrel, he will make a good profit. By selling December oil future contracts at the current December price (75 USD), he can lock in that good profit and eliminate the fluctuation in price, or price risk.

In December, let's suppose the price of oil has dropped to 70 USD per barrel in the Spot market. The oil producer delivers his oil in the Spot market and receives 70 USD. However, he held a short position at 75 USD, and with the final settlement price at 70 USD, he made a futures trading profit of 5 USD per barrel. Therefore, his net selling price is

75 USD, which he locked in earlier. 70 USD (Spot sale) + 5 USD (futures trading profit) = 75 USD (per barrel).

What if the price went higher? Let's suppose the price of oil has increased to 83 USD per barrel in the Spot market. The oil producer delivers the oil in the Spot market and receives 83 USD. However, he held a short position at 75 USD, and with the final settlement price at 83 USD, he incurs a futures trading loss of 8 USD. His net selling price is still 75 USD, which he locked in earlier. 83 USD (Spot sale) − 8 USD (futures trading loss) = 75 USD (per barrel).

Oil—long hedge

Airlines use jet fuel, a major cost, which closely correlates to the price of crude oil. Therefore, airlines can lock in their cost by buying oil futures—a long hedge.

The concept and logic for an airline buying oil futures contracts is the same as the food wholesaler buying corn futures contracts. In order to better understand this, work out the numbers where the price is 75 USD and subsequently moves higher and lower.

When you think about these events, whoever is responsible for the purchase of raw materials or any commodities that a company needs can have a major impact on that company's profitability or its lack of profits.

These are facts. In the U.S., during the first quarter of 2008, only one airline, Southwest Airlines, made a profit. It's been well documented that the main (and perhaps only) reason for this was that this airline projected a dramatic increase in the price of oil. They hedged/locked in their jet fuel costs, at the equivalent of crude oil prices of 51 USD per barrel. Later, when other airlines were paying for jet fuel at the equivalent of crude oil at 100 to 140+ USD, Southwest Airlines was paying for their fuel at the equivalent crude oil price of 51 USD. The CEO probably took most of the credit for their profitability, but whoever was responsible for purchasing was the real hero.

For long and short hedgers of many commodities, the use of storage facilities can smooth out the precise contract months that contracts are bought or sold. For example, a hedger, such as a crude oil producer, who thinks the price of oil will decrease significantly in the future, can sell many oil futures contracts and lock in a price that may reflect many, many months of production.

When hedging (long or short), as you actually participate (by buying or selling) in the Cash market, you will liquidate an equivalent number of contracts in the futures market.

Other hedges

A cotton grower can hedge or eliminate the risk of fluctuations of his selling price in the same manner as the wheat farmer with a short hedge. A clothing manufacturer who uses cotton can hedge or eliminate the risk of fluctuations of his purchase price in the same manner as the food wholesaler with a long hedge.

I was in Jamaica, presenting my workshop, when a government official spoke to me about how chickens are a food staple there. The price of corn, the main food for chickens, had been steadily increasing, causing the chicken growers to continually raise the selling price of their chickens to a point where many people could not afford to buy chickens. A real potential crisis.

We discussed how futures could help, through a cooperative or with government assistance. If it was likely that the price of corn would continue to rise, the potential profits of buying corn futures would offset the rising cost of chickens. We also talked about how, for this situation, buying corn Call options (as we'll see later) would probably be a better alternative. Clearly, it was an enlightening moment.

CHAPTER 4

Hedging Stock Portfolios

The opportunity to hedge stock portfolios is available to both institutional asset managers and retail individuals who own securities. In some countries hedging is more easily understood if it is referred to as insurance.

In order to show examples of hedging, we first have to make some assumptions.

Assume that our stock exchange has a stock index, which we'll call the Composite Index (CI), and 1 CI futures contract = index value × 100 USD. (This would be defined in the contract specifications).

Assuming the current value of CI = 1200, then 1 CI futures contract = 120,000 USD (1200 × 100 = 120,000) value.

Therefore, every contract bought or sold would be equivalent to buying or selling 120,000 USD of stock market value.

Let's also assume you are a portfolio manager (also called a fund or asset manager) with a stock portfolio of 25 million USD.

Let's suppose you are a little bearish on the market and want to hedge your portfolio 20%. This means that you do not want the risk of 100% of your portfolio, but only 80%.

How can you do this?

Answer: You can accomplish this by using futures contracts. 20% of 25 million USD = 5 million USD. Since each CI contract has a current value of 120,000 USD, 5 million ÷ 120,000 = 42 contracts. (There are no partial contracts, so there must be some rounding off).

Therefore, the manager should sell 42 CI futures contracts, which have a current market value of approximately 5 million USD.

The manager is long 25 million USD of market value in the cash (or stock) market and short 5 million USD of market value in the futures market. In reality, he now has a market risk position of a (net) long position of 20 million USD.

If the market goes up, he should be making a profit on his 25 million USD stock portfolio, but he'll incur a loss on his 5 million USD short futures position.

If the market goes down, his portfolio loss on his 25 million USD portfolio would be hedged or partially offset by a profit on his 5 million USD short futures position. The asset manager's specific stock portfolio would probably not move (up or down) with the exact same magnitude as the stock index, so his hedge would probably not be exactly as anticipated. However, it is still a valid hedge. For example, if his stocks did slightly better—say, 2%—than the stock index (meaning that his portfolio loss was 2% less than the index when the stock market went down), then his overall net loss would be applicable to the equivalent of 78% (not 80%) of his portfolio.

Let's now assume that the portfolio manager is totally bearish on the stock market, and would like to get out of the equity market completely. It would be difficult to sell everything, especially if the markets are thin. He will still want to collect dividends, and he also thinks that his portfolio should do better than the overall market. Also, if he's a pension or mutual fund manager, he is probably still getting contributions or fund deposits.

He can hedge 100% of his portfolio by selling (25 million ÷ 120,000 =) 208 CI futures contracts.

I have an equity manager friend who has always been hedged 100%. As he receives more money contributions, he sells equivalent (in value) S&P index futures contracts. He doesn't care whether the stock market goes up or down. As long as his stock selection outperforms the overall stock market, he makes money. If it underperforms, he loses money.

In an up market, he'll make a net profit if the profits in his portfolio are greater than the loss he will incur on his short futures position. In a down market, he'll make a profit if the losses in his portfolio are less than the profits on his short futures position.

CHAPTER 5

Hedging Debt Portfolios

Bond or debt portfolio managers would use the exact same methodology to hedge their portfolios as described in the previous chapter.

This would presume that there is a short-term debt index (such as U.S. Treasury, or "T-bill") futures contract, which in the US, is a 90-day debt instrument, and/or a long-term debt index (such as the U.S. Treasury or Government bond "T-bond") futures contract, which in the US, is a 30-year debt instrument.

On futures exchanges, debt futures traditionally trade based upon price, not interest rate. This means as interest rates go up, bond prices go down.

Short- and long-term rates and debt instruments are relative. Short-term rate instruments may be 30 days, 90 days, or the like. Long-term rates may be 5 years, 10 years, 30 years, etc. When hedging, the futures contract should have the same approximate maturity or debt life as the cash market debt portfolio.

Let's assume you want to hedge a bond or long-term debt portfolio. You would do so for the same reasons that an equity manager would want to hedge his portfolio. The concept and methodology are the same as for equities.

If you anticipate long-term rates will be increasing, this means that you anticipate bond prices will decline. To hedge against this possible event, you would sell bond futures. If bond prices do go down, although you will be losing money in your cash portfolio, you will be offsetting this loss with profits on your short futures position.

If you anticipate long-term rates will be decreasing (meaning that bond prices will increase), you will probably not hedge at all.

Assume 1 government bond futures contract = 100,000 USD par value. Let's assume a bond fund manager with a 20 million USD bond portfolio wants to hedge or remove the market risk of 25% of his portfolio.

Since 25% of 20 million USD = 5 million USD, the bond fund manager will sell or go short (5,000,000 ÷ 100,000 =) 50 T-bond futures contracts.

The bond manager will have an overall or net market risk of 75% of his portfolio, rather than a 100% market risk. If the debt market prices go up (bond prices increase and rates decrease), his 100% cash portfolio gains will be somewhat offset by his short futures position (of 25% of his cash portfolio) losses. If the debt market goes down (bond prices decrease and rates increase), his 100% cash portfolio losses will be somewhat offset by his short futures position (of 25% of his cash portfolio) profits.

Treasury bonds are conservative (as opposed to risky) investments. At contract expiration, the futures and cash market price for T-bonds will be the same. Therefore, these T-bond futures have the same risk and volatility, and are just as speculative or conservative as T-bonds that trade in the cash market.

The same situation and methodology is true for short-term debt (T-bill) futures contracts.

Assume 1 T-bill futures contract = 1,000,000 USD par value.

To hedge 30% of a 30 million USD short-term debt portfolio, sell or go short 9 T-bill futures contracts.

30% of 30 million USD = 9 million USD, and since each contract is 1 million USD, the portfolio manager should sell 9 contracts.

The exact same reduced market risk will prevail.

CHAPTER 6

Pre-positioning for Asset Managers

Assume you manage a large pension fund of stocks, short-term debt, or long-term debt, or a combination of security types. Also, assume that there are regular or periodic contributions, and from the payroll data, you will know when and approximately how much money will be contributed.

Let's assume you think equity prices will increase, so you would want to buy stocks now. Although you will buy the stocks at a later time at higher levels when the money is contributed, you can lock in the current price levels by buying stock index futures now.

If our Consolidated Index (CI) future has a current value of 120,000 USD, and you are to receive a pension fund contribution of 800,000 USD at a later date, you should buy 6 CI futures contracts (6 × 120,000 = 720,000 USD. There are no partial contracts, so you will buy either 6 or 7 contracts), and establish a long futures position. This is the equivalent value of the fund deposits that you will be receiving. (Of course, you'll have to make the appropriate margin deposit).

Now, as the contributions are made, you buy the specific stocks on the stock exchange that you want, and sell the equivalent amount of CI futures contracts at the same time, reducing your long futures position. The increased prices (from the time you made this decision) that you will be paying for the specific stocks that you buy would be offset by the profit realized on your long CI futures position. You therefore locked in the approximate cost of the stocks that you purchased. This is known as pre-positioning.

If the stock market went down, although you would have saved money by buying the specific stocks at a lower price than you thought, you would have realized a loss on your long CI futures position. Regardless of the market's subsequent movement, you locked in the approximate overall net cost for the 800,000 USD of stocks purchased.

As mentioned before, this is not 100% precise because the securities you eventually buy will probably not move in the exact same percentage (up or down) as the index future. However, it's a hedge that reduces subsequent price movement risk, and could reduce 90% or more of the price risk.

If your stock exchange trades futures on individual stocks, then one would pre-position by buying the specific stock futures in advance of the actual stock purchases (selling the futures position as the stocks are purchased), thus rendering a much more precise pre-positioning outcome.

You would use the exact same methodology if you wanted to pre-position a bond purchase. For example, for the same 800,000 USD anticipated fund contribution, if the bond futures index (assuming there is one) is at 97 (or 97% of par value), because Bond futures contracts are at 100,000 USD, you would buy 8 bond futures contracts (800,000 USD ÷ 97,000 USD = 8.2). In the same manner, you would sell/reduce your futures position as the fund contributions are received and bonds are bought in the cash market.

CHAPTER 7

Other Hedging and Spread Trading Applications

Currency hedge

Suppose a very large corporation, headquartered in the U.S., has offices in Europe, and is required to pay his European staff in euros.

If the Treasurer thinks that by the time he has to meet his payroll, the euro will be getting stronger against the USD, and he wants to lock in the current rate, he will buy euro futures contracts now. Euro futures contracts trade versus the USD, so only a single transaction will be required. If there are 125,000 euros per futures contract, and the European payroll is 500,000 euros, then he should buy 4 euro futures contracts (500,000 ÷ 125,000 = 4). Thus, he will lock in his payroll requirement. If he is correct, and the euro does get stronger (relative to the USD), then he has saved his company money by paying fewer USD now for the same amount of euros that he would have to purchase later.

Of course, if the euro subsequently got weaker (versus the USD), then the company would have been better off if they had not hedged. But that's always the case. A hedge locks in a rate or price, thus eliminating subsequent market price fluctuation risks, whether or not the subsequent market movements are in your favor.

Interest rate spread trading

With many commodities, there are fundamental relationships that have been tracked and projected. Traders, arbitrageurs, and interested individuals have studied these relationship patterns and do their trading accordingly.

I'll assume there is a long-term interest rate futures contract (e.g., U.S. Treasury bond or T-bond) and a short-term interest rate futures contract (e.g., U.S. Treasury bill or T-bill). There has been a relationship between long-term and short-term interest rates, with long-term interest rates being higher than short-term interest rates. Long-term and short-term interest rates tend to rise and fall together, but the acceleration and timing of these movements vary.

Based upon the current T-bond and T-bill market rates, if you think that the current (rate) spread or gap is wider (i.e., the difference between the T-bond and T-bill rates is greater) than it should be, and you think that the spread will be narrowing, you may want to take advantage of this opportunity.

Remember, as bond or debt prices go up, interest rates go down. To do this, you would buy T-bond futures (expecting the price to rise and the rate to fall) and sell T-bill futures (expecting the price to drop and the rate to rise).

You would make these trades in the same contract months.

Depending upon the exchange trading system, this may be accomplished as a single "spread" trade.

As with all spread trades of this nature, it doesn't matter whether the rates go up or down. The relationship between the rates is the only profitability criterion. It is still a speculative trade, but certainly more conservative and with less risk than taking an outright long or short position on either interest rate futures contract.

If you are correct, the T-bond interest rate will drop in relation to the T-bill rate, thus narrowing the spread, and you'll have a net profit. However, if you are wrong and the rate spread widens further, you will incur a net loss.

If you think the interest rate spread or gap will widen, you will do the reverse trades—sell the T-bond future and buy the T-bill future.

Other inter-commodity spread trading

These are buy and sell transactions involving two different commodities.

Precious metals are a good example of this type of spread trading. There has been an historic relationship between gold and platinum, with platinum having the higher value. As with long and short interest rates, the price of these metals tend to go up and down together, but not necessarily at the same amount or rate.

As with the interest rate spread, if you think the spread or gap in price between these two metals will *narrow*, then buy gold futures and sell platinum futures. If correct, the higher price metal (platinum) will not increase as much as gold or decrease more than gold (depending upon if precious metal prices rose or fell).

If you think the spread will *widen*, then do the opposite— sell gold and buy platinum.

Again, what determines whether or not you have a profit or loss is the rate or amount that these metals move relative to each other.

There are other good examples of intercommodity spread trading, such as using currency futures.

Currencies always trade against another currency. Just to mention a few, the euro, the British pound (BP), the Japanese yen, the Canadian dollar, and others trade versus the U.S. dollar. Because of this situation, you can do a spread trade by only executing one side—buy or sell.

Let's look at the BP versus the USD. Perhaps you think that the BP will get stronger than the USD. This means that in the future you think that it will take more USD to purchase the BP. Since the BP trades versus the USD already, you will just buy BP futures.

If you think the USD will get stronger versus the BP, then sell BP futures contracts.

If you are an asset manager and are holding securities in foreign currencies, then the profitability of that position is dependent upon both:

1. The price movement of that security

2. The fluctuation between the foreign currency and your own currency

The foreign currency aspect can be hedged or negated by selling futures in that foreign currency.

All of these currency spreads work best if we are dealing with hard currencies, such as the ones indicated above. Otherwise, it is a more complicated process.

Intra-commodity spread trading

These are buy and sell transactions involving the same commodity, but different months. For these types of trades, there is always a Near month and a Far month.

Agricultural commodities (e.g., wheat or corn) are good examples of this type of trading. In these situations, the Far month future has a higher price attributable primarily to the costs of storage, insurance, and financing for the time frame between the contract months.

Whether you think these costs will increase or decrease determines the spread position that you will take. There may be other factors that affect your decision, but, for example, if you think these costs will increase, meaning you think the spread will widen, then you will buy contracts of the higher-priced Far month, and sell contracts of the Near month.

Of course, if you think the spread will narrow, you do the opposite—sell the Far month and buy the Near month futures contracts.

As the overall conditions of supply, demand, and other factors affect the price of wheat, corn, or other such commodities, the price for all months of the same commodity future will move in the same direction, but not necessarily at the same rate. However, you don't care whether the prices go higher or lower. It's only the relationship between the Near and Far months that matter.

On most commodity or futures exchanges, there are usually traders that deal specifically in spread trades, referred to as "spread traders." They act as dealers, and as such they normally make two-way markets in the spreads, indicating both a bid and an offer in which they are willing to "buy the spread" or "sell the spread" of the specific Near and Far months of a given commodity.

Maintaining a futures position

When a futures contract expires at the end of the contract month, there is no more trading in that commodity month. What if you have a long (or short) position in a particular commodity month that is expiring, and wish to maintain that position? How do you do that? Of course, you knew the answer would be, "It's easy."

Simply roll out that position by doing a spread trade. For example, suppose you think the stock market will continue to go higher, and you are already long the September (Sep) stock index future, and the next contract month is December (Dec). Prior to the Sep expiration, do a spread trade, selling the Sep futures contracts and buying the Dec futures contracts.

After that execution, your Sep position will be flat and you will be long the Dec stock index future contract(s).

CHAPTER 8

FCMs and IBs

FCMs are Futures Commission Merchants. They are analogous to stock brokerage firms that are also Clearing Members (CMs) of a stock exchange depository. They trade and settle futures contracts.

FCMs "carry" institutional and retail customer accounts. This means that they maintain customer account records, hold the customers' cash deposits, and are responsible for the accounting of customers' futures and options positions.

To be an FCM, the firm must have adequate capital and operational capabilities in accordance with the rules of the depository, which is similar to being a CM of the stock exchange depository.

IBs are Introducing Brokers. They are full members of the stock exchange and enjoy all of its trading privileges, but are not members (CMs) of the depository.

IBs contact customers and do business with them, but they do *not* carry customer accounts. They hold no customer funds, and since they are not depository members, they are not responsible for maintaining the customers' positions or records. They introduce their customers to FCMs. One can think of IBs as branch offices of large stock brokerage firms.

There will be a business relationship and financial arrangement between the FCM and the IB. The IB might be paying for trade execution services, but the IB will certainly be paying for the FCM's clearing and recordkeeping services. The financial arrangement may be based upon per trade or per order, trading volume, a percentage of the commission that the IB is charging the customer, a combination of a fixed amount and a variable charge for activity, and by other means as well.

Almost always, the IB will be required to have an escrow deposit with the FCM to protect the FCM in case there are any customer defaults or non-payments. It is the IB that is bringing the customer to the FCM and has the contacts with the customer, and it is the IB that should be responsible for any customer malfeasance.

Legally customers are the customers of the FCM, not the IB.

CHAPTER 9

How Futures Operate

Trading

Trading can happen electronically, as for stocks, or via Open Outcry, as on the commodity exchanges in the U.S. From a customer's perspective, electronic trading is far superior to Open Outcry. In this book, we'll only discuss electronic trading, which is the recommended approach.

The electronic trading system that stock exchanges use in most countries is certainly adequate as a start. That system could be adapted to accommodate futures and options.

The same matching rules and criteria would prevail.

Although there would be commonality for the same commodity, each commodity month would be treated as a separate identity. This would be analogous to identifying a preferred stock and a common stock of the same company—they are separate identities.

The order types would be basically the same as for stocks—market orders, limit orders, day orders, good till cancelled (GTC), all or none (AON), fill or kill (FOK), etc. Whatever the stock exchange system is currently using would be adequate.

There may be market orders for execution only near the close of business, during the Closing Range. A common end-of-day order is the Market On Close (MOC) order, a buy or sell market order that must be executed within the Closing Range. This type of order is usually entered when a customer does not or will not have the margin requirements to maintain a position overnight, and therefore wants to get out of that position by the end of the day.

Using the U.S. Open Outcry trading system on commodity exchanges, in my tenure as a CEO of a futures brokerage firm, I never witnessed a customer Buy MOC order that did not get executed at the highest price within the Closing Range or a Sell MOC order that did not get executed at the lowest price within the Closing Range. This gave new meaning to MOC orders, depending upon your point of view. For floor brokers, MOC means Mercedes On Close, and for customers MOC means Murder On Close.

Stop orders. If this type of order is not within the current trading system, in order to adequately trade futures, stock exchanges should modify its system to accommodate "Stop orders" (and even Stop limit orders). For stock exchanges, these orders are not as critical, and they may not have this capability. Although Fundamental Analysis is utilized by commodity traders, Technical Analysis is used extensively, and Stop orders are absolutely necessary, especially when trading many different commodities.[2]

A brief explanation of the uses of Stop orders is appropriate.

Stop orders are used to limit a loss or protect a profit in a position. For example, if you buy a futures contract at 20, and you want to limit your loss to approximately 10%—which means you want to sell the contract if the price drops to 18—you would enter a Sell Stop order at 18. If the contract trades at 18 or the best bid is at 18, your order becomes a Sell market order. A Stop Limit order will identify a price limit. You may enter a Stop order at 18, limit at 17½. This means that if the contract trades at 18 or the best bid is at 18, your order becomes a Sell Limit order at 17½.

You may have initially purchased a futures contract at 10, and it is now trading at 20. With the same Stop orders

---

[2] Investment and trading decisions based upon Fundamental Analysis deal with analyzing the fundamentals of a company, such as sales, earnings. market share, etc., or commodity, such as supply, demand, costs, etc. Technical Analysis deals with analyzing price and volume trading patterns, such as determining resistance and support levels, of a company or commodity.

stated above (placing a Sell Stop order at 18), you can protect a profit of approximately 8 points. As the contract price moves higher, you will probably want to raise your Stop orders, canceling the current order and placing one with a higher stop price, thus protecting a bigger profit.

Stop orders are also used to establish a position. Suppose a futures contract is trading in the high 20s range. Based upon your Technical Analysis, the "resistance level" for this contract is 30, which means that if the price breaks (exceeds) 30, its upside potential is high. Since you don't know if it will ever break 30, you will not buy it now. However, if the price does break 30, you will want to buy that futures contract. To accomplish this, you enter a Buy Stop at, say, 30½. This means that if the contract trades or is offered at that price, your order becomes a Buy market order.

Short sales. As previously indicated, another significant difference between stocks and these derivatives is in the area of short sales. With derivatives, there are no rules or restrictions regarding short sales. All long and short sell orders are entered in the same manner, and the resultant execution will result in the creation of a short position or a reduction of a long position. Therefore, your stock exchange trading system should be modified to bypass or eliminate any checks or validations for accepting long sell orders and short sell orders.

Settlement

Here we have some significant differences.

With stock trading, the settlement date is usually anywhere from 1 day to several days after trade date. With futures, the margin settlement of all trades are (in the morning of trade date +1) prior to the opening of trading the next day. (Actual settlement of the contract delivery versus payment is in the future, when the contract expires.)

For stock trading, on settlement date, the full value of the trade is delivered (by the seller) and paid for (by the buyer) through the depository settlement system. With derivatives, there is no delivery or payment between buyer and seller. For all trades and existing long and short positions, a "good faith" or margin deposit would be made by the Clearing Members to the depository.

In order to perform the margin analysis on a customer basis, in addition to the contract month positions, the depository must maintain money balances for each account, similar to the depositories currently maintaining customer stock position balances. (In the US, neither customer stock nor money balances are maintained by its depository, DTC.)

The depository system must maintain both long and short positions for each commodity month traded. For all accounts, for each contract month, the total number of contracts long must equal the total number of contracts short.

The settlement price for each commodity contract month is the price to which all open positions are valued. The settlement price may be the same formula or algorithm for determining the settlement or closing price for stocks. For example, the weighted average of the last 15 or 30 minutes of trading would be an appropriate determination. This time frame is the Closing Range. This formula may be the same for all commodities traded on the exchange, or may vary by commodity. The formula will be stated in the contract specifications for each commodity.

CHAPTER 10

Margin

Margin is the deposit that a Clearing Member (CM) makes with the depository based upon the value of the open positions that the CM is holding for all of his customer accounts. The positions of other brokerage firms (IBs) that a CM clears for are also included.

Based upon the value of their trades and open positions, all customers are required to deposit adequate margin with the CM.

All margin requirements are stipulated in the contract specifications. The margin requirements are established by the exchange and approved by the regulator.

Margin requirements are designed to reflect and satisfy the financial (risk) exposure of positions taken.

For every CM, there are 2 components of margin: initial and variation. The sum of both margin types represents the daily total margin requirement for each CM.

1. Initial Margin (IM)

As defined in the contract specifications, Initial Margin deposits will be in cash and/or securities, if permitted. If securities are permitted, it is usually only government securities.

- IM is charged on a per contract basis for all contracts, long and short, by commodity and month.

- IM tends to be approximately 10% to 15% of the value of the futures contract. Usually the volatility of the commodity is one of the major considerations for the IM amount. There are available methods, such as SPAN or TIMS, which can be used to determine the IM. Sometimes the IM is based upon a 2-day maximum loss, which is the equivalent of the price limit for 2 days.

- Every Clearing Member, based upon his total closing positions, must deposit the required IM prior to the next day of trading.

- IM requirements for the CM are either on a net basis, the net of long and short positions for each contract month, or on a gross basis, reflecting the positions held by each customer (by each contract month). Futures exchanges use both methods.

- As conditions warrant, the exchange may change its margin requirements.

2. Variation Margin (VM)

The VM always settles in cash.

- VM is applicable to all CMs and institutional customer accounts.

- VM is the daily valuation difference of trades and open positions to the settlement price. This is known as "marking to market."

- For the depository, the total daily VM of all CMs equals zero, a zero sum game.

- The sum of the daily IM and VM amounts results in a "net pay or collect" for each CM.

- Therefore, CMs and their institutional customers settle (pay or collect) the unrealized profit or loss daily. The IM for the positions they hold remain with the depository.

Maintenance Margin (MM)

A retail customer will also have an IM requirement (which he deposits with his CM), which may be different than the IM for CMs and institutional accounts. This retail IM requirement will be higher, and stated in the contract specifications.

For retail customers, it is not practical to settle VM requirements with his CM on a daily basis, so instead of VM, there is a Maintenance Margin (MM) requirement. The MM is the level of equity that the customer must maintain. For example, a retail IM may be 15%, and the MM may be 10%.

Retail customers will be entitled to, and should receive at their request, any "excess" margin in their account due to profits (for their positions, which are marked to market) and a reduction in their IM due to a reduced position.

Using the above IM and MM requirements, if a contract has a value of approximately 10,000 USD, then the IM will be stated as 1,500 USD and the MM will be 1,000 USD.

Other Margins

There are also Spread Margins, which are Initial Margin amounts for inter-commodity and intra-commodity spreads. Spread Margins are stated on a per spread contract basis in the contract specifications. Since the risk is less (for 2 spread contracts) than for having an outright long or short position (of 2 contracts) in a commodity, the Spread Margin will be less than the Initial Margin for the same number of one-sided contracts. The Spread Margin may even be less than the margin for a single side contract.

An exchange (together with the clearinghouse or depository) may impose a Special Margin, and it may be for only the buy or sell side. There may also be an Additional Margin instituted for both sides. These are usually temporary, reacting to an unusual condition.

Near the expiration of a contract (month), the exchange may impose a Pre-expiry Margin. This is usually when there is a physical delivery involved. It gives greater assurance that the delivery will be made and paid for. It tends to reduce or eliminate the positions of speculators at that time. Additional Delivery Margins may also be imposed.

For reasons previously stated, all commodities should have position limits. If there is an "undue concentration" by a broker or customer for a commodity or a single commodity month (the position exceeds a certain percentage of the Open Interest), the exchange may impose an additional Concentration Margin.

CHAPTER 11

Overview of IT Implications for Trading and Settlement of Derivatives on Stock Exchanges

Regarding the major IT implications for modifying a stock exchange system to accommodate these derivatives, below are some of the basic systems similarities and differences.

The input formats, computer screens, and report formats would be the same. This is even more desirable than would be the case if a totally new derivatives system is installed. The brokers and CMs would already be oriented to the various reports and how to access meaningful customer information and other data.

For the trading system, a current stock exchange system is adequate—a good start:

- Same order matching criteria

- Quantities are stated as number of contracts rather than number of shares.

- With derivatives, there will be no rules or checking for short sales.

- Derivative system must accommodate Stop orders.

- With derivatives each commodity contract month is a separate identifier, analogous to a separate security identifier.

- At contract expiration, no further trading is permitted, and that particular contract month is deleted from the trading system.

The settlement system is significantly different.

- With derivatives, there is no daily settlement of delivery and full value payment for trades previously executed.

- Positions held are stated as number of contracts rather than number of shares.

- The Depository system must be modified to record and maintain ("carry") short positions. The total number of long contracts held must be the same as the total number of short contracts.

- Unlike for stock processing, the depository system must hold money amounts since the depository is responsible for calculating and collecting the (initial and variation) margin requirements of the CMs and disbursing excess margin amounts to the CMs (for their customers) on a daily basis.

- At contract expiration, for physical deliveries, the depository must pair-off the outstanding long and short positions for the delivery of the contract.

CHAPTER 12

Developing Leveraged Products

As stock exchanges seek more business and activity, and more financial opportunities to offer its members and their customers, they can establish leveraged trading for their listed stocks. There are essentially two different approaches to take.

- Margin trading and short selling versus futures (and options) on individual securities

We can make these alternatives more comparable if the margin rates are the same, giving both alternatives the same leverage. Futures tend to have significantly lesser margin requirements than traditional margin trading. However, an exchange can set the Initial Margin rate for futures at 50%

of the contract value, and a Maintenance Margin level of 35% equity—approximately the same margin rates for stocks traded on stock exchanges.

Let's first look at the major advantages of selecting margin trading and short selling over futures trading. With margin trading and short selling:

- Buyers receive all corporate actions—primarily cash and stock dividends and voting rights.

- If you own securities, you may loan them to short sellers and earn interest income on the value of the loan.

- As a borrower, you may receive a share of the interest income as a rebate.

- There would be no need to modify the trading and settlement systems.

- A stock borrowing / lending system must be established.

Now let's look at the major advantages of selecting futures trading over margin trading and short selling. With futures:

- You have the ability to hedge. Asset managers may reduce (or even eliminate) market risk by selling stock or bond index futures, and also eliminate currency risk for foreign securities held.

- An asset manager may pre-position or take advantage of "buying the market" or buying specific security futures before actually buying specific securities.

- Customers pay no interest on the difference between the value of a purchase and the cash deposit made. (The notion of paying interest on a debit balance does not exist). Brokerage firms may view this as a disadvantage, in that customer debit balance interest income can be a significant source of revenue.

- Rather than selecting individual stocks, customers can buy or sell "the entire market" by buying or selling the stock index future.

- By settling the futures contract deliveries for cash, short squeezes can be avoided.

- For the depository or for individual brokerage firms (as in the U.S.), there is no need to develop a lending/borrowing control system. This would be a major undertaking, as it would also have to include the control of corporate actions between borrowers and lenders.

- Once futures are established, a whole new array of financial products can be offered by expanding into other commodity futures.

Chapter 13

Options

Introduction

Options are much more complicated and complex than futures. Options are traded on many commodities—financial (stocks, bonds, stock indices, currencies, etc.) and many others (metals, crude oil, agricultural, coffee, etc.). Options are traded in both the Cash market and Futures markets. For example, there are options on stock indexes and stock index futures. There are options on government bonds and government bond futures.

There are two types of options contracts—Calls and Puts.

A *Call* contract is an option, but not an obligation, to Buy a specific quantity of a specific underlying commodity at a specific price (referred to as the strike or exercise price) within a specific time period.

A *Put* contract is an option, but not an obligation, to Sell a specific quantity of a specific underlying commodity at a specific price (referred to as the strike or exercise price) within a specific time period.

Options are "decaying assets." At expiration, they are worthless, and their value is zero.

Option trading

As with futures, options trade in contracts, and the quantity of a trade refers to the number of contracts.

Regarding trading systems, options have the same basic characteristics as futures.

Also like futures, all aspects of the Put or Call option are defined in the contract specifications, such as the size or quantity of the commodity (e.g. as 100 shares of a specific stock, 100,000 USD of government bond (par value), 125,000 euros, 1,000 barrels of crude oil, or 100 ounces of a specific fineness of gold).

As you can see, the quantities are aligned with that of corresponding futures contracts. The same is true for the contract expiration months.

Strike or exercise price

This is the price at which the option—Put or Call—is exercised. (The terms "strike price" and "exercise price" are synonymous). For Calls, this is the price at which the owner or holder of the Call option will pay if and when he exercises his option to buy or "Call" the specific underlying commodity. For Puts, this is the price at which the owner or holder of the Put option will receive if and when he exercises his option to sell or "Put" the specific underlying commodity.

Each strike price and each contract month expiration is treated as a separate identity, just like a different stock.

For example, the contracts for Sep crude oil 30 Call, Sep crude oil 30 Put, Sep crude oil 40 Call, and Sep crude oil 40 Put are treated as 4 separate trading and settlement entities.

The meaning of options for buyers and sellers:

For buyers

The buyer or holder of an option has the privilege, or option. He may or may not *exercise* this privilege. It is not a commitment. The buyer pays (an amount) for this option or privilege, which is referred to as the premium.

Upon exercise, the holder of a Call option will receive (versus payment) the underlying spot or futures commodity.

Also, at his discretion, the holder of a Put option will deliver (versus payment) the underlying spot or futures commodity

If the option strike price is *below* the current market price, the holder of a Call option will exercise the option (or merely sell the Call in the market) and realize a trading profit.

If the option strike price is *above* the current market price, the holder of a Call option will *not* exercise the option. The holder would not want to pay the strike price for that underlying commodity or futures position when he can buy it in the market at a lower price.

The same is true for Put options, except the strike price and current market price situations are reversed. For example, if the option strike price is *above* the current market price, the holder of a Put option will exercise the option (or merely sell the Put in the market) and realize a trading profit.

For sellers

The seller or writer of a Put option is obligated to *receive* the underlying commodity if and when a holder exercises his option, and to pay the strike price to the holder.

The seller or writer of a Call option is obligated to *deliver* the underlying commodity if and when a holder exercises, and to collect the strike price from the holder.

Option sellers (or writers) receive the premium payment from the buyers, and therefore earn income and interest from the premiums collected. That's why they write the options.

Chapter 14

Option Operations

Trading and Settlement

Option trades should be executed electronically with the same system, types of orders and trade match criteria as futures.

Also as with futures, there is no delivery versus payment on trade settlement date. There is a daily margin calculation, which would be calculated by the depository for its Clearing Members.

Option margins

For *buyers*: There are *no* margin requirements for buyers of Puts or Calls. The buyer pays the entire premium, and there is no further downside risk exposure.

For *sellers*: The exchange would set the minimum requirement for its Clearing Members. Clearing Members may impose a higher rate to its customers.

Although described more fully in a subsequent chapter, covered options are when the seller has the underlying position in his account and naked options are when the seller does not have the underlying positon.

- For covered (Put or Call) options: The margin requirement would usually be the underlying commodity or its full value equivalent, which is calculated daily.

- For naked (Put or Call) options: This would vary with Clearing Members, but a typical margin requirement would be the option premium collected + 20% of the underlying commodity value, which is calculated daily.

Option delivery—exercise and assignments

Deliveries are only made versus payment at the "option" or decision of the option holder.

As with futures, the delivery details are defined in the contract specifications. Deliveries may be Physical (the underlying commodity) as they traditionally are in the US, or in Cash. Both methods are used.

Call options will be exercised as long as the strike price is less than the underlying spot or futures price. This means the option has value. (For Put options, the price relationship is opposite).

It should be noted that the underlying commodity for an option in the Spot market is the Spot commodity (e.g., government bond), whereas an option in the futures market is a futures position (e.g., government bond futures position on that futures exchange). Regarding options on futures, upon exercise, the holder of a Call option on a futures contract would now have a long futures position of that contract. Upon exercise, the holder of a Put option on a futures contract would now have a short futures position of that contract. The writer or seller of those options would have the opposite positions.

When a holder wishes to exercise his option, his Clearing Member notifies the depository. The depository then "assigns" that option to a customer with a short position. In some countries, the exercise of options is only permitted at expiration.

As part of the exchange and depository rules, assignments to short positions are usually based upon age or on a random selection.

At expiration, as with futures, there is no further trading for all strike price options for that month.

As mentioned above, at expiration, the option has no value. Of course, there is no time value and the option holder losses his full premium. If there is intrinsic value, the system may (and should) automatically pay this value to the holders (from the writers). This leads us into the topic of Option values and pricing.

CHAPTER 15

Option Pricing

The option price is the option premium. The terms are synonymous.

Option price = intrinsic value + time value

Intrinsic value equals the "in the money" amount.

In the money. This is the price difference between the market price and the strike price when the market price of a *Call* option is *higher* than the strike price, or when the market price of a *Put* option is *lower* than the strike price.

Out of the money. This is the price difference between the market price and the strike price when the market price of a *Call* option is *lower* than the strike price, or when the market price of a *Put* option is *higher* than the strike price.

At the money. When the market price of a Call option or a Put option is at the strike price.

Some examples of intrinsic value are:

If Dec Crude Oil is trading at 37 USD per barrel,

Dec Crude Oil 35 Calls are 2 USD in the money, and its intrinsic value is 2 USD.

Dec Crude Oil 35 Puts are 2 USD out of the money, and it has no intrinsic value.

Dec Crude Oil 40 Calls are 3 USD out of the money, and it has no intrinsic value.

Dec Crude Oil 40 Puts are 3 USD in the money, and its intrinsic value is 3 USD.

Dec Crude Oil 37 Calls are at the money, and it has no intrinsic value.

Time value is the value of the option based upon formulas and analysis of the commodity's price history. This analysis considers the time remaining until contract expiration + the price volatility + how near or close the strike price is to the market price. All of these factors affect the time value component, but the good news is that you don't have to figure this out. There are formulas or models, such as Black and Scholes, which are universally accepted. Without getting into the mathematics or analysis of the volatility (and its beta coefficients) or the closeness of the strike price to the market price, we know that the more time is left until contract expiration, the higher this component of the time value will be.

The market's determination of the time value is simply the difference between the premium price and the intrinsic value. If the option is trading out of the money or at the money, there is no intrinsic value, so the time value is the total premium.

CHAPTER 16

Trading and Benefits of Options

Options are like insurance: you pay a premium, and you become protected.

Buying a Call (of a security) is analogous to buying the security except that because of the premium that you paid, there is *no* downside market risk.

You also have a great amount of leverage. For example, suppose a stock is trading at 53. Instead of buying the stock at 53, you paid a 5-point premium for a 50 Call option. (Your option has an intrinsic value of 3 points, and therefore its time value is 2 points).

Suppose the price of the stock goes to 58. If you bought the stock, you would have a 5-point profit or a 9% (5 ÷ 53 = 9.4) return on your investment.

Your 50 Call would probably be selling at 9 even if the time value decreased to 1, since the intrinsic value is now 8. Since your investment (the premium) was 5, the return of a 4-point profit would be 80% (4 ÷ 5), which is much better than 9%.

That is leverage. You paid a small percentage of the value of the underlying commodity. If you bought the stock in a securities margin account, you would be paying interest on your debit balance, which represents the financing your broker charged for lending you the balance between the cost of your purchase and your margin deposit. Buying the Call option not only provides much leverage, but there are also no interest charges to your account because no money is borrowed.

The big plus is that you have market downside protection. If the market price goes down, you simply don't exercise your Call option. Therefore, your maximum loss would be limited to the premium you paid.

If at expiration the stock price dropped to 52, there would be no time value, but your Call would still be worth 2 points of intrinsic value, so instead of losing your entire premium of 5 points, you would have a 3-point loss instead, which would be a significant loss of 60% of your investment.

Buying a Put option is analogous to selling a security short. As in the case of a Call, you have *no* market risk beyond your premium payment (here the protection or insurance is against a rise in the market price), and there are also no interest payments.

Further downside protection

If you have a long stock position or a long futures position, you can protect against a price decline if you buy Puts. For the Put that you buy, the lower the strike price, the lower the premium you will pay—but the less protection you will have.

You can also protect yourself against a price increase if you have a short stock position or a short futures position by buying Calls. Also, for the Call that you buy, the higher the strike price, the lower the premium you will pay, but the less protection you will have.

Writing or selling options

The terms "writing" and "selling" are synonymous. There are two types of options that one can write: naked or covered.

Writing a *naked option* means that the seller does *not* own the underlying commodity. (Institutional investors are usually not permitted to do this.) This would be analogous to selling short—selling something that you do not own.

Writing a *covered option* means that the seller owns the underlying commodity. Typically, if someone owns a stock (cash or futures), they would write a Call. If someone is short a cash or futures position, they would write a Put.

People write naked and covered options in order to collect the cash premiums and to earn additional interest income on the cash collected.

Common strategy: writing covered options

A common strategy is for investors to write covered Call options. If you are long a stock (or futures position) and are thinking about selling by writing a Call instead, you would collect a premium.

If the stock price goes higher, the stock will be Called away from you. However, you were thinking about selling the stock anyway, and with this strategy, you collected additional funds (the premium).

The flip side is that if the stock goes down, the Call would not be exercised against you. You would have collected a premium, but now you would still own the stock, which is at a lower price. In this scenario, consideration would be given as to when one might liquidate both the stock and option positions, which would be to buy the Call and sell the stock. It becomes a matter of comparing the income from the collected premium against the subsequent paper loss.

The same strategy for writing Call options could also be used for long stock futures positions.

By writing Calls against long stock or futures positions, although you collect premium income and earn additional interest income, you do not participate in further price appreciation because the stock or futures position will be Called away from you.

Other strategies: Writing naked options

Someone might write a naked Call option if he had an opinion that the price of the underlying (stock or other commodity) would go down. If he is correct, and the price does decline, then the Call would not be exercised and the writer would have collected the full premium. The same situation exists for Put options, but in the reverse market direction.

Here's another strategy for writing naked options. It allows an investor to buy stock, or any futures contract, at a net cost below the current market or at a discount. Suppose you would like to buy a stock that is trading at 10. You could write a Put on that stock at 10 and collect the premium (for example, of 1 point). If the stock trades at less than 10, it will be Put to you, meaning that you will own the stock at 10. However, since you collected a 1-point premium, your net cost is 9, a 10% discount from where you initially wanted to buy it. If the stock price goes higher, the option will not be exercised and you will keep the premium, but you will not have benefited from the stock's appreciated price (had you bought it). I happen to know one investor who usually buys stock in this manner. He estimates that approximately 75% of the time the stock does go higher, so he keeps the premium, and he is pleased with that result. It becomes a matter of investing conservatively or aggressively.

As you can see from the examples throughout this book, there is no free lunch.

Offsets

Buying a Put does *not* offset buying a Call. If you did that for the same commodity month, and some people do, you would now have two positions.

You would be paying 2 premiums, and you would make money or a net profit if the price of the underlying moved in either direction more than the cost of the 2 premiums.

Buying a Put and selling a Call is also *not* an offset. You have compounded your position because both positions are bearish, meaning that both positions will profit if there is a price decline, and both positions will lose money if there is a price increase.

Likewise, buying a Call and selling a Put is *not* an offset. You have compounded your position, since both positions are bullish, meaning that both positions will profit if there is a price increase, and both positions will lose money if there is a price decrease.

It is important for investment and brokerage firm officers to be aware of how their traders and asset managers are using these derivatives and when positions are being reduced or compounded.

I have known traders who say, "You can only die once." This means that if you are stuck with a loss that will no doubt cost a lot of the firm's money and your job, by compounding your position, if the market turns in your favor, you will be OK. If not, there's not much difference in being bankrupt by a small amount or a large amount. You are out of business in either case. Management must be diligent in monitoring these situations.

"Option heaven"

Because of the high leverage and no further downside market risk beyond the premium, buying options appear to be a very attractive trading strategy. However, a very high percentage of options never get exercised and expire with no value. Although these statistics are several years old, in the United States, expired options amounted to more than 80%. In Korea, which trades more stock index options than any other exchange, an exchange officer told me that more than 90% of the options never get exercised. This means that the buyers, usually retail customers, are losing their premiums, and the writers, usually the institutions, are earning the premium income. The exchange official attributed this high leverage trading to the gambling nature of Asians and were very concerned that these losses present a potential major social problem. As such, they are considering somehow changing the contract specifications to ameliorate this situation.

CHAPTER 17

Hedging with Options

We already saw how leverage helps facilitate the option speculator. Options also benefit hedgers.

We'll use the same illustrations as we did with futures. Again, it doesn't matter if the delivery of the option is for Cash or for the Physical underlying commodity.

Farmers can hedge or protect against a decline in prices for their agricultural product (e.g., wheat) with options. A farmer can do this by buying wheat Put option contracts. Of course, the farmer must pay a premium for this protection. (That is why buying options is sometimes referred to as "insurance.") For the added cost of the premium, rather than being locked in to his selling price (as with futures), the farmer is in a win-win situation. He will exercise his Put option if there is a decline in the price of wheat, selling his crop at the strike price (of the options contract). If there is an increase in price, the farmer will *not* exercise his option (let it expire), and sell his wheat at the higher Spot market price.

In the exact same manner, the oil producer will hedge against a market price decline by buying crude oil Put option contracts. The oil producer will exercise his Put options if the price declined, but would not exercise if there was a price increase.

The same logic and situation is true for Call options. To protect against an increase in wheat prices, a food wholesaler (a buyer of wheat) would buy wheat Call option contracts. If the price of wheat increases, he would exercise his option and buy the wheat at the Call strike price. If the price declines, he would simply not exercise his option and buy the wheat at the lower spot price.

In the exact same manner, to hedge against an increase in oil prices, an oil refinery (a buyer of crude oil) will buy crude oil Call option contracts. The method and logic as to whether or not to exercise the option are the same as the food wholesaler.

In a similar manner, institutional and retail customers can use options to hedge or buy insurance for their portfolios. Let's assume there are options on a stock (or bond) index, but not on individual stocks (or bonds). To protect against a decline in equity (or debt) market prices, one would buy

Put options on the index. If the overall market price (or index) went up, his portfolio would presumably increase in value, and he would not exercise the option. However, if the market price went down, he would sell his Put option at the strike price. The profit generated by this transaction would primarily be the difference in intrinsic value (between his purchase and sale of the option. Remember, as the market price declines, the intrinsic value of a Put option increases).

If there are options traded on individual stocks, and a customer wants to hedge his ownership position in that stock against a decline in price, he will buy a Put option in that stock. Again, if the market price for that stock increases, he will not exercise the option. However, if the market price declines, he can either sell the Put option, as above, and obtain a profit on the option, or he can buy the stock (at the current lower price) and exercise his Put option, selling or "putting" it at the (higher) strike price.

Let's assume we have options on individual stocks. If a customer buys (or owns) a stock at 50, he can protect or insure that position by buying a Put option for that stock at 50. Let's assume the option premium is 3. As stated above, if the stock price goes higher, he has a profit on his stock position, and he lets his option expire. Of course, to have an overall profit, the stock price must exceed 53, his overall cost including the option premium. If the stock price goes lower, he will make the exact same profit on his Put option as he will lose on his stock position, meaning he has downside protection. In order to maintain that protection, the customer will have to buy another Put option when the current one expires.

The same is true in the opposite direction. Let's assume we have options on individual stock futures. Suppose a customer sells (goes short) a stock futures contract at 40. He can protect or insure that position by buying a Call option for that stock future at 40. Again, let's assume the option premium is 3. If the stock futures price goes lower, he has a profit on his futures position, and he lets his option expire. Of course, to have an overall profit, the stock futures price must decline below 37, his overall short sale proceeds (40) less the cost of the Call option (3). If the stock futures price goes higher, he will make the exact same profit on his Call option as he will lose on his stock futures position, meaning he has downside market protection. Similarly, in order to maintain that protection, the customer will have to buy another Call option when the current one expires.

If we have options on stock indexes, a portfolio manager or anyone can protect or hedge his investment by "buying downside insurance." The investor can protect all or part of his portfolio by buying Put options on the stock index in an amount that equals the protection that he seeks. For example, if he has a portfolio of 20 million USD and wants to hedge or protect 50% of his portfolio (he's somewhat bearish on the overall market), he will buy Put options on the stock index whose total stock index value amounts to 10 million USD. The strike price that the investor selects (for the purchase of the Put options) will determine the option premium that he will pay (the higher the strike price, the higher the cost of the Put option). This allows the investor to choose the amount and level of protection that he wants.

In summary, the difference between hedging against adverse price movements with futures versus hedging with options is that with futures, the price is locked in; with options, you are also protected against adverse price movements by paying a premium (i.e., insurance). However, you still benefit from a price movement in your favor.

CHAPTER 18

Options Helping the Farmer and the People

Governments are using options to assist their nations' economies and social conditions. Here are a few examples.

In Mexico, the government has assisted the farmers by enabling them to avoid the risk of a price decline for their crop at harvest time, when they sell their crops in the marketplace. The government bought Put options for them. This stabilized or locked in their selling price. If the spot price when their product is sold is lower than the strike price, the farmers will exercise their option and deliver their produce at the strike (higher) price. Thus, the government has guaranteed the delivery price. Of course, if the spot price is higher than the strike price, the farmer will not exercise the option, and he will deliver his crop at the higher price.

Even if the delivery is for cash, the farmers' profits from exercising the Put options will offset the lower price that they will receive when delivering their crops in the Spot market. Educating the farmers about this program was a major undertaking, and was vital to its success.

In India, which is primarily an agrarian economy, the farmers are very dependent upon the amount of annual rainfall it receives. If the rainfall is not adequate, many farmers cannot grow enough crops to support their families, and the suicide rate among the farmers greatly increases. This has presented a very real social problem. Education would be a major undertaking, but government officials and the exchanges are exploring how potential profits on rainfall futures or Put options would offset the reduced farming income for the farmer in times of inadequate rainfall. As of this writing, a rainfall index has been established, and the commodity exchange is waiting for government approval to trade indices and options.

In Jamaica, where I presented my workshop on derivatives, I was informed by a government staff person that because of the increasing price of corn (the primary feed for chickens), chicken prices were increasing dramatically to a point where many families could not afford to buy this food staple. This has created a real concern for the government. I suggested that either via a community cooperative or with government assistance, buying corn futures (which I mentioned before) or Call options would create trading profits that would offset the increased cost of chickens. Sometimes it really helps to think outside the box. As of this writing, derivatives are not being traded here, but whenever they do commence trading, these types of applications will probably be given serious consideration.

CHAPTER 19

Review of Uses and Choices

Futures versus options

Futures and Options are similar in that they both provide a great deal of leverage for speculators, and both can be used to hedge stock and other cash market positions.

They are different in that with futures there is downside market risk (for buyers and sellers), but with buying options, there is no downside market risk. The risk is limited to the premium that is paid. Option sellers have market risk.

Option sellers receive additional (premium) income, but would not participate in a favorable market movement.

Except for the modifications previously described, a stock exchange could use their current system for futures trading and options trading.

Regarding settlement, with both financial instruments, there is no daily delivery versus payment process as there is for stocks. For futures, there are margin requirements that must be met by both long and short position holders. For options, only the short positions are required to meet margin requirements.

Regarding deliveries, delivery at the end of each contract month expiration can be for Cash or Physical (the underlying commodity). If physical deliveries are utilized, for futures, all net long and short positions are paired off. With options, where deliveries take place holders' discretion, the short positions would be assigned by the depository.

In emerging countries, the stock exchange depositories usually maintain the positions of all customer accounts. This practice should also be adopted for futures and options, and would include maintaining money balances as well. (It is not this way in the U.S.)

The concept of Open Interest is the same for options and for futures. With both financial instruments, there is no primary market, and the equal number of contracts in long and short positions are only established when buy and sell orders are matched on the exchange.

Regulatory concerns

I have intentionally not addressed the regulatory issues and concerns for initiating futures and options trading on stock exchanges in this book, but they would be comparable to those of a stock exchange. I think that any country that has a stock exchange and is preparing to launch derivative trading should have the same government regulator and structure for this new activity.

The regulator's focus should be on customer protection, and that would be demonstrated with an adequate examination and enforcement program of the exchanges and its members, and a diligent market and customer surveillance program.

CHAPTER 20

Recommendations for Moving Onward

There are several important steps to be taken for a stock exchange to launch derivative trading and settlement. These following tasks can be performed concurrently, and should be initially directed towards trading futures contracts.

- Establish regulatory and exchange trading and settlement rules, oversight, surveillance, and enforcement procedures.

- Educate and train participants—regulators, exchange and depository staff, brokerage firm personnel, and even potential customers.

- Establish trading and settlement systems. This would probably mean adapting the current stock exchange systems.

- Establish a customer back office recordkeeping, accounting, and reporting system. This would mean that a current service provider would modify its customer accounting and reporting system (to accommodate these derivatives) and make it available to brokerage firms and depository Clearing Members. This is an undertaking that the depository may want to consider.

- Establish the futures contracts to be traded. This would involve an economic analysis of the most appropriate contracts to trade. The exchange should seek the assistance of acknowledged economists in order to determine the specific commodity contracts to trade. Of course, legal assistance would also be required.

It would appear that the leading types of contracts to consider when initiating derivative trading on the exchange would be:

- a stock index future on the exchange's primary index

- a bond or debt index future

- agricultural and other futures (such as oil, cotton, wheat, precious metals, etc.) that are most relevant to the country's economy

- consider the trading of stock index futures of indices of stock exchanges in the region

- appropriate currencies and other commodity futures

- after futures are launched and operative, consider establishing option contracts for the most active futures contracts and/or on individual stocks.

- To expand the prominence and influence of this stock exchange, once this activity is launched, other stock exchanges in the region can link up with this exchange, making it the derivatives exchange for the entire region. This can be achieved with the other participating exchanges not having to modify their current trading and settlement systems.

www.ingramcontent.com/pod-product-compliance
Lightning Source LLC
Chambersburg PA
CBHW030815180526
45163CB00003B/1289